Discover the Wonders of
SEDONA

Lovely Scenics by Season • Birds, Mammals, Reptiles • Ruins & Parks • Geology

By Suzanne Clemenz

Suzanne Clemenz chose Sedona as her home in 1976. For 23 years she and her late husband Bob travelled as freelance scenic photographers, working with dozens of publishers. After Bob's passing, Suzanne continued photographing and expanded her freelance writing talents.

Over the years, Suzanne's comprehension of Sedona's allures grew beyond its obviously stunning geology. Eventually she wanted to share her discoveries with Sedona's visitors, residents, and students. This book is her way of doing so.

Chapters of seasonal scenic images are followed by chapters depicting natural wonders such as plants or birds associated with those seasons. Chapters with scenic autumn and winter vistas are followed by chapters about topics that are most comfortably explored in cooler seasons, though you can keep exploring in hotter months by heading outdoors between daybreak and late morning.

Sedona offers much more than visual splendor. With this book you'll discover many smaller wonders that can enrich your visit -- or a lifetime -- in Sedona's Red Rock Country.

Contributors:
Gary Romig, *bird and animal art*
Ray & Joanne Reed, *additional flower photographs*
Paul Lindberg, *geology chapter*
Christopher Picknally, *graphic design*

Published by:
Clemenz PhotoGraphics, Inc., Sedona, AZ 86351 • sm.clemenz7@suddenlink.com

ISBN: 978-0-615-83610-2   Printed in Taiwan

Table of contents

Acknowledgements

Thanks to friends and family who gave me encouragement, facts and feedback in preparing this book. Of special note are Pamela Chionis, Dena Greenwood, Vidyananda Whiton, and the staff and volunteers at Sedona's U.S. Forest Service Ranger Station.

References

A Field Guide to the Plants of Arizona, by Anne and Lewis Epple, Falcon Press
Shrubs and Trees of the Southwest Uplands, by Francis H. Elmore, Southwest Parks and Monuments Assn.
Common Plants of the Verde Valley & Sedona, www.naturesongs.com/vvplants
Geology strata graphic: *arizonaruins.com/Sedona*
So, Why Are the Rocks Red, by Mike Ward
Sedona Through Time, Wayne Ranney

Front cover: *Cathedral Rock glows in evening light. With B. Clemenz*
Inside front cover: *Clearing snow clouds dance around Fin Rock.*
Right: *A Century plant (agave) stands sentinel at Breadloaf Butte in Red Canyon*

SPRING

The appearance of manzanita blossoms, like strings of miniature Oriental lanterns, heralds spring's arrival in February. The temperatures are frequently perfect for hiking, although occasional dustings of snow occur well into April. Rather than the gradual warming temperatures characteristic of spring elsewhere, the weather often alternates -- a few mild, summer-like days interspersed with a few cold, windy, winter-like days. The skies are seldom gray for more than two days, bathing budding plants with perfect doses of precipitation and sunlight.

Above: "Manzanita" refers to these blossoms, shaped like "little apples."

Right: Spring in Oak Creek Canyon's West Fork brings wildflowers and Painted Redstarts.

Following: In rare years May can bring blankets of Owl clover along F.S. 152C. With B Clemenz

Birders flock to places like Page Springs Fish Hatchery and Sedona Wetlands Preserve to observe the waning numbers of waterfowl and the return of tanagers, orioles, warblers, and the dramatic Common Black hawk. Even in town the air is filled with a chorus of birds staking out their nesting territories.

Besides the wildflowers peeping from many natural nooks, crannies and fields, Sedona's highways and streets are a froth of blossoming fruit trees, flowers and bulbs. The backdrop of red cliffs and earth gives blossoms an extra zing. Even the cacti, which look unfriendly in other seasons, fling out their gaudy petals in a welcoming embrace to the bees and hummingbirds, who wallow in the pollen.

Above: Desert willows cover themselves with clusters of orchid-like blossoms.

Right: The geometrical lines of the Chapel of the Holy Cross are softened by flowering fruit trees.

Left: At Crescent Moon Ranch Day Use Area the cottonwoods, ashes and willows show a haze of green leaves below Cathedral Rock. The white-barked Arizona sycamore shows off its late-leafing physique for a few more weeks.

Spring and fall are great months for hiking the trails. Minimize mud and ice encounters by choosing sunnier trails and waiting a couple of days after precipitation. The old saying around here, in the middle of a downpour, is, "Wait 15 minutes and the dust will be blowing." Figuratively speaking, of course. But local mud can be extra-slippery.

Any wild mammals you encounter may have young ones with them. Keep your camera ready, and keep a safe distance from protective four-legged parents.

Pioneer families found Sedona's climate and iron-rich soil perfect for apples, apricots, cherries, pears, plums, nuts and many vegetables. Slide Rock State Park continues the apple orchard started by the Pendley family in the early 1900s. Today many a Sedona yard sports fruit trees and, at the least, tomato and squash plants. There are wild walnut trees in Oak Creek Canyon, and also Himalaya blackberries that escaped from pioneer gardens. The settlers, like us, took time for picnics, hikes and spring planting.

Left: *Slide Rock State Park was the Pendley Homestead's orchard for decades before becoming a park in 1987.*

Below: *Pointleaf manzanita and smooth-bark Arizona cypress intertwine in Secret Canyon.*

Rufous Hummingbird • *Selasphorus rufus*

Bird life is rich in the Sedona area because habitats are diverse: a river and several creeks; marshes; grasslands; chaparral; forests of pinyon - juniper, Ponderosa-oak, and spruce-fir; canyons and mountains; ranch lands, neighborhoods, and developed wetlands. No wonder many birds migrate through, stop to breed, or reside here year 'round.

296 bird species have been recorded in Sedona and Verde Valley. This chapter illustrates 116 commonly seen species and lists another 40 (not in strict taxonomic order.) Birds are shown in relative size within each grouping, though not with other groupings on a page. Make a mark beside each species you see, and watch your list grow!

Bird artist Gary Romig digitally photographs a species' correct habitat, and then draws the bird in minute detail on computer, in its habitat. The following pages show his bird art without their habitats. To see them with their backgrounds, like the Rufous hummingbirds above, visit **artofbirds.com**.

Visit **northernarizonaaudubon.org**. Join their many field trips and learn about other birding events such as the Verde Valley Nature Festival (April,) and regularly scheduled guided bird walks at local birdy places.

HABITAT CODES: Ae *Aerial;* **CR** *Chaparral/rocky slopes;* **Dv** *Developed lands;* **ML** *Multiple habitats;* **MG** *Mesquite/Grasslands;* **MW** *Marshes/Wetlands;*

WATERFOWL

		Habitat	Size	Season
	Duck, Bufflehead	Wa	13"	W
	Duck, Canvasback	Wa	21"	W
1	**Duck, Mallard**	**Wa**	**23"**	**R**
	Duck, No. Pintail	Wa	25"	W
	Duck, No. Shoveller	Wa	19"	W
2	**Duck, Ring-necked**	**Wa**	**17"**	**W**
3	**Duck, Ruddy**	**Wa**	**15"**	**W**
4	**Duck, Wood**	**Wa**	**18"**	**R**
5	**Gadwall**	**Wa**	**20"**	**W**
6	**Goose, Canada**	**Wa, Dv**	**27"**	**W**
7	**Grebe, Pied-billed**	**Wa**	**12"**	**R**
	Gull, Ring-billed	Wa	19"	M
8	**Merganser, Common**	**Wa**	**25"**	**W**
	Teal, Cinnamon	Wa,	16"	W
9	**Teal, Green winged**	**Wa**	**14"**	**W**
10	**Widgeon, American**	**Wa**	**19"**	**W**

BIRDS OF PREY

		Habitat	Size	Season
1	**Eagle, Bald**	**Rp**	**31"**	**W**
2	**Eagle, Golden**	**MG**	**30"**	**W**
3	**Falcon, Peregrine**	**Ae**	**17"**	**B**
4	**Kestrel, American**	**Ae**	**10"**	**R**
5	**Harrier, Northern**	**MG,MW**	**18"**	**W**
6	**Hawk, Common black**	**Rp**	**20"**	**B**
7	**Hawk, Cooper's**	**Rp, PO**	**16"**	**R**
	Hawk Ferruginous	MG	23"	W
8	**Hawk, Red-tailed**	**Ae**	**19"**	**R**
	Hawk, Sharp-shinned	Ml, Dv	11"	W
	Hawk, Zone-tailed	Rp	20"	B
	Osprey	Wa, Rp	23"	M
9	**Vulture, Turkey**	**Ae**	**26"**	**B**

WADING, MARSH & SHORE BIRDS

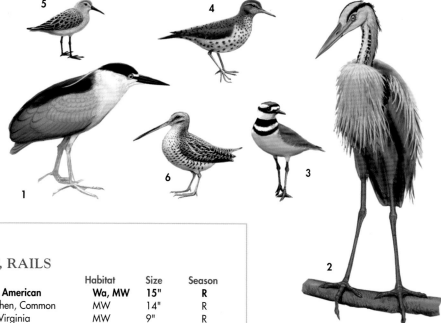

		Habitat	Size	Season
1	**Heron, Black-crn night**	**Wa, Rp**	**25"**	**B**
2	**Heron, Great blue**	**Wa, Rp**	**47"**	**R**
	Heron, Green	MW	19"	B
	Ibis, White-faced	Wa, MW	23"	W
3	**Killdeer**	**MW**	**10"**	**W**
	Sandpiper, Least	MW	6"	M
4	**Sandpiper, Spotted**	**MW**	**7"**	**W**
5	**Sandpiper, Western**	**MW**	**6"**	**M**
6	**Snipe, Common**	**MW**	**10"**	**W**
	Yellowlegs, Lesser	MW	10"	W

COOT, RAILS

		Habitat	Size	Season
1	**Coot, American**	**Wa, MW**	**15"**	**R**
	Moorhen, Common	MW	14"	R
	Rail, Virginia	MW	9"	R
2	**Sora**	**MW**	**9"**	**R**

American Coot: r

Sora: r

QUAIL, DOVES, PIGEONS

		Habitat	Size	Season
1	**Dove, Band-tailed pigeon**	**PO, Dv**	**14"**	**B**
	Dove, Eurasian collared	Dv	11"	R
2	**Dove, Inca**	**MG, Dv**	**8"**	**R**
3	**Dove, Mourning dove**	**MG, Dv**	**12"**	**R**
	Dove, Rock (Pigeon)	Dv	13"	R
4	**Quail, Gambel's**	**MG, Dv**	**11"**	**R**

HUMMINGBIRDS

		Habitat	Size	Season
1	**Hummingbird, Anna's**	**Dv, Rp**	**4"**	**R**
2	**Hummingbird, Black-chinned**	**Dv, Rp**	**4"**	**B**
	Hummingbird, Broad-tailed	Dv, Rp	4"	B
3	**Hummingbird, Rufous**	**Dv, Rp**	**4"**	**M**

CUCKOO & OWLS

		Habitat	Size	Season
1	**Owl, Great Horned**	**ML**	**23"**	**R**
2	**Owl, Northern pygmy**	**Rp, Pd**	**7"**	**R**
3	**Roadrunner**	**MG, Dv**	**23"**	**R**

KINGFISHER & DIPPER

		Habitat	Size	Season
	Dipper, American	Wa	7"	R
1	**Kingfisher, Belted**	**Wa**	**13"**	**R**

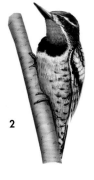

WOODPECKERS

		Habitat	Size	Season
1	**Northern Flicker**	**PO, Rp**	**12"**	**R**
2	**Sapsucker, Red-naped**	**PO, PJ**	**9"**	**W**
3	**Woodpecker, Gila**	**ML**	**9"**	**R**
	Woodpecker, Hairy	PO, Rp	9"	R
4	**Woodpecker,** **Ladder-backed**	**ML**	**7"**	**R**

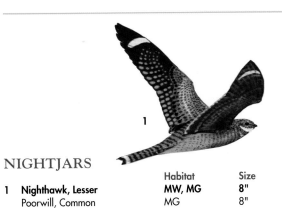

NIGHTJARS

		Habitat	Size	Season
1	**Nighthawk, Lesser**	**MW, MG**	**8"**	**B**
	Poorwill, Common	MG	8"	B

HABITAT CODES: Ae *Aerial;* **CR** *Chaparral/rocky slopes;* **Dv** *Developed lands;* **ML** *Multiple habitats;* **MG** *Mesquite/Grasslands;* **MW** *Marshes/Wetlands;*

FLYCATCHERS

		Habitat	Size	Season
1	**Flycatchers, Ash-throated**	MG	8"	B
2	**Flycatchers, Brown-crstd**	Rp	9"	B
	Flycatcher, Cordilleran	Rp	5"	M
	Flycatcher, Gray	MG	6"	B
3	**Flycatcher, Vermillion**	Rp	6"	B
4	**Kingbird, Cassin's**	Rp	6"	W
5	**Kingbird, Western**	MG	8"	B
	Peewee, Western wood	PO	6"	B
6	**Phainopeppla**	PJ, Rp	8"	B
7	**Phoebe, Black**	Wa	7"	R
8	**Phoebe, Say's**	MG,PJ	7"	R

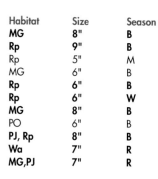

SWALLOWS & SWIFT

		Habitat	Size	Season
	Swallow, Barn	MG	7"	M
1	**Swallow, Cliff**	Wa, Dv	5"	B
2	**Swallow, No. rough-wing**	Wa	5"	B
	Swallow, Tree	Rp	5"	M
3	**Swallow, Violet-green**	PO	5"	B
	Swift, White-throated	Ae	6"	B

LARK & PIPIT

		Habitat	Size	Season
1	**Lark, Horned**	MG	7"	W
	Pipit, American	Rp,Dv	6"	W

SHRIKE & MOCKINGBIRD

		Habitat	Size	Season
1	**Shrike, Logger-headed**	PJ, MG	10"	W
2	**Mockingbird, Northern**	MG, Dv	10"	B

JAYS & RAVEN

		Habitat	Size	Season
	Jay, Pinyon	PJ	10"	W
1	**Jay, Stellar's**	PO, Dv	11"	R
2	**Jay, Western scrub**	ML	11"	R
3	**Raven, Common**	ML	25"	R

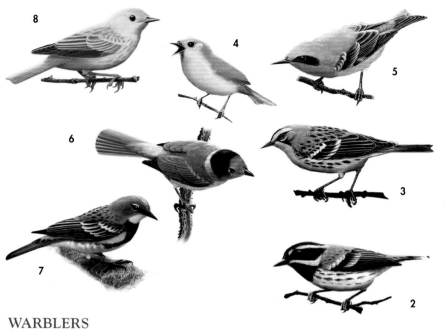

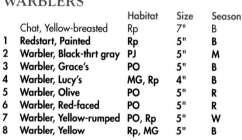

WARBLERS

		Habitat	Size	Season
	Chat, Yellow-breasted	Rp	7"	B
1	Redstart, Painted	Rp	5"	B
2	Warbler, Black-thrt gray	PJ	5"	M
3	Warbler, Grace's	PO	5"	B
4	Warbler, Lucy's	MG, Rp	4"	B
5	Warbler, Olive	PO	5"	R
6	Warbler, Red-faced	PO	5"	R
7	Warbler, Yellow-rumped	PO, Rp	5"	W
8	Warbler, Yellow	Rp, MG	5"	B

NUTHATCHES & CREEPER

		Habitat	Size	Season
	Creeper, Brown	PO	5"	R
	Nuthatch, Pygmy	PO	4"	R
	Nuthatch, Red-breasted	PO	4"	W
1	Nuthatch, White-breasted	PO, Rp	5"	R

VIREOS & KINGLET

		Habitat	Size	Season
1	Kinglet, Ruby-crowned	Rp, PO	4"	W
2	Vireo, Plumbeous	Rp, PO	5"	B
3	Vireo, Hutton's	Rp, PO	4"	R
4	Vireo, Warbling	Rp	5"	B
5	Vireo, Bell's	MG, Rp	4"	B

TANAGERS

		Habitat	Size	Season
1	Tanager, Hepatic	PO	8"	B
2	Tanager, Summer	RP	7"	B
3	Tanager, Western	PO	7"	B

SPARROWS

		Habitat	Size	Season
1	**Sparrow, Black-chinned**	**PJ**	**5"**	**R**
2	**Sparrow, Black-throated**	**MG**	**5"**	**B**
	Sparrow, Brewer's	MG	5"	W
3	**Sparrow, Chipping**	**MG**	**5"**	**W**
	Sparrow, Fox	PJ	7"	W
4	**Sparrow, House**	**Dv**	**6"**	**R**
5	**Sparrow, Junco, Oregon**	**ML**	**6"**	**W**
	Sparrow, Lark	MG	6"	W
6	**Sparrow, Lincoln's**	**Rp**	**5"**	**W**
	Sparrow, Rufous-crowned	CR	6"	M
	Sparrow, Sage	MG	6"	W
	Sparrow, Savannah	MG, Dv	5"	W
7	**Sparrow, Song**	**Rp**	**6"**	**R**
8	**Sparrow, White-crowned**	**ML**	**7"**	**W**
	Sparrow, White-throated	Rp	6"	W
	Sparrow, Vesper	MG	6"	W

GROSBEAKS, CARDINAL, BUNTINGS

		Habitat	Size	Season
	Bunting, Indigo	Rp	5"	B
1	**Bunting, Lazuli**	**Rp**	**5"**	**M**
2	**Cardinal, Northern**	**Rp, Dv**	**9"**	**R**
3	**Grosbeak, Black-headed**	**Rp, Dv**	**8"**	**M**
4	**Grosbeak, Blue**	**Rp, MG**	**7"**	**B**

BLACKBIRDS , COWBIRDS, GRACKLE

		Habitat	Size	Season
1	**Blackbird, Brewer's**	**Dv, MG**	**9"**	**W**
2	**Blackbird, Red-winged**	**MW**	**9"**	**R**
	Blackbird, Yellow-headed	MW	10"	M
	Cowbird, Bronzed	Dv	8"	B
	Cowbird, Brown-headed	Dv, MG	7"	B
3	**Grackle, Great-tailed**	**Rp, Dv**	**16"**	**R**

HABITAT CODES: Ae *Aerial;* **CR** *Chaparral/rocky slopes;* **Dv** *Developed lands;* **ML** *Multiple habitats;* **MG** *Mesquite/Grasslands;* **MW** *Marshes/Wetlands;*

TOWHEES

		Habitat	Size	Season
1	Towhee, Abert's	**Rp**	**9"**	**R**
2	Towhee, Canyon	**MG,CR**	**8"**	**R**
	Towhee, Green-tailed	MG, Rp	7"	M
13	Towhee, Spotted	**PJ**	**8"**	**R**

FINCHES

		Habitat	Size	Season
	Crossbill, Red	PO	6"	W
	Finch, Cassin's	PO	6"	W
1	Finch, House	**Dv,ML**	**6"**	**R**
	Goldfinch, American	Dv, Rp	5"	W
2	Goldfinch, Lesser	**Rp,Dv**	**4"**	**R**
	Siskin, Pine	Dv, PJ	5"	W

MEADOWLARK, ORIOLES

		Habitat	Size	Season
1	Meadowlark, Western	**MG**	**9"**	**R**
2	Oriole, Hooded	**Rp,Dv**	**8"**	**B**
3	Oriole, Bullock's	**Rp**	**8"**	**B**
	Oriole, Scott's	PJ, MG	10"	B

STARLING

		Habitat	Size	Season
1	Starling, European	**ML**	**8"**	**R**

SUMMER

Double rainbows occur somewhere in Sedona on many days when it rains at sunset. Catching one over Cathedral Rock at Crescent Moon Ranch Day Use Area is especially magical.

Summer's monsoon rains visit Sedona almost daily mid-July to mid-September. Days often start out clear, with scout clouds appearing late morning. By mid-afternoon battalions of towering cumulus clouds raucously scour the earth with thunder and lightning, wind and rain. Then, their energies spent, they linger on in exuberant sunsets. Cool, balmy nights are so rain-washed clear that the Milky Way flings a visible banner across the black velvet sky.

Above: Monsoon clouds create pinto shadows beyond the needle's eye on Schnebly Hill Road.

Left: Watercress floats on Oak Creek Canyon's cool waters.

Right: Agaves (Century plants) can blossom as late as mid-July.

The sediments which comprise Sedona's sandstone and limestone rock formations eroded over eons into the cliffs, buttes, turrets and hoodoos we see today. Some resemble familiar objects such as a bell, cathedral domes and spires, courthouse columns, even a merry-go-round. It's a fun quest to find and photograph them.

Page 24, left top: Snoopy Rock reclines on a ridge east of Uptown.

Left middle: The Mittens are between Jordan Rd. and Soldier Pass Rd.

Left bottom: Elephant Rock is just south of Morgan Rd. east of Hwy. 179.

Right top: Castle Rock is the north backdrop of many Village of Oak Creek neighborhoods.

Right bottom: The Bench parallels a lower portion of Schnebly Hill Road.

This page, top: Bell Rock is hand-bell shaped and rises almost 500' above the surrounding grasslands beside Hwy. 179.

Right: Coffee Pot Rock is at the east end of the ridge that forms West Sedona's backdrop.

Too many hikers become casualties. Check weather reports before hiking. Stay near water, campgrounds, or in shady canyons. Carry a cell phone and flashlight for signaling. Stay put if lost!

It can get blazin' hot out there, folks, plus or minus 100°F. Dehydration, sunburn, and hiking our high elevations deplete even very fit people. Wear a sun hat. Use sunscreen. Avoid flash floods. Carry at least a gallon of water per person, per day and drink it! Pour some over your head and shirt for evaporative cooling.

Never hike alone. Tell someone your destination and expected return time. Our Search & Rescue crews deal daily with folks, including athletic young people, who ignore basic safety. Survivors often say they knew better.

Left: *West of town off Dry Creek Road are many trails in the Red Rock - Secret Mountain Wilderness.*

Left Bottom: *Oak Creek is spring fed and cool even on hot summer days.*

Right: *A girl braces for her first trip through slippery-as-soap Slide Rock.*

Below: *Slide Rock State Park combines local history with refreshing water fun in Oak Creek Canyon.*

Summer lingers through September in Sedona. It cools down enough for a short, spectacular hike through Fay Canyon, and for folklorico dancers to twirl and tap at a Tlaquepaque fiesta. Green apples form at Slide Rock State Park, and the monsoon showers wane. Cool breezes and chillier evenings herald autumn, another season of visual banquets. You're invited to return for that feast!

Above: *Folklorico dancers at Fiesta del Tlaquepaque.*

Right: *Monsoon clouds paint a new picture around Cathedral Rock on many summer evenings.*

PLANT LIFE

The Sedona - Verde Valley (Arizona's Central Basin) has average annual rainfall of 17 inches, so it is not a desert. Instead, it encompasses life zones ranging from mesquite grasslands (up to 4,000',) the pinyon-juniper belt, the pine-oak belt, and even a bit of the spruce-fir belt (around 6,000'.) If botany is a major interest of yours, great references are listed on page 2. But many visitors are simply curious about the area's most commonly-seen flowers, shrubs, trees, and cacti, and this chapter will provide many answers.

Often plants from adjoining life zones mingle at the edges of elevation changes. After some 40 years here I'm still discovering botanical surprises everywhere from canyon forests to rocky slopes.

Tear your eyes away from the red rocks and discover Sedona's many botanical wonders, some seasonal, some perennial.

Right: Schnebly Hill Road passes through plant zones ranging from Pinyon/Juniper, to Spruce/Fir.

Left: Desert Willow in bloom.

Bottom right: Palmer's penstemon on Schnebly Hill Road.

Bladderpod, Gordon's
Lesquerella gordonii
to 16", MG, by R & J Reed

Cardinal Flower
Lobelia cardinalis
to 5', RP, by R & J Reed

Columbine, Golden
Aquilegia crysantha
to 4', RP by R & J Reed

Daisy, Blackfoot
Melampodium leucanthum
to 20", MG

Datura, Sacred
Datura meteloides
to 4', MG

Fleabane, Aspen
Erigeron macranthus
to 2', PO

Flour o'clocks, Desert
Mirabilis multiflora
to 2', MG

Globemallow, Desert
Sphaeralcea ambigua
to 40", MG

Marigold, Desert
Baileya Multiradiata
to 2', MG

MG = mesquite/grasslands **RP** = riparian (near water) **RS** = chaparral/rocky slopes **PJ** - pinyon/juniper **PO** - pine/oak **SF** spruce/fir

Nightshade, Silverleaf
Solanum eleagnifolium
to 3', MG

Owl Clover
Orthocarpus purpurascens
to 16", MG

Penstemon, Eatoni
Penstemon eatoni
to 2', stems purplish, MG

Penstemon, Golden beard
Penstemon barbatus
to 4', PO

Penstemon, Palmer's
Penstemon palmeri
to 5', RS

Penstemon, Parry's
Penstemon parryi
to 4' , RS

Poppy, Mexican gold
Eschscholtzia mexicana
to 16", MG

Poppy, Prickly
Argemone pleiacantha
to 3' MG

Scarlet Bugler
Penstemon subulatus
to 3', RS by R & J Reed

Sunflower, Common
Helianthus annuus
to 9', MG

Verbena, Goodding's
Glandularia gooddingii
to 12", MG by R & J Reed

You will find many more lovely flowers than are shown here. Many festoon some of the shrubs shown in the following section. Some bloom quite early, and even in winter Desert Broom shrubs look as if they're covered with fluffy white blossoms. Ask for a plants list at a Ranger Station.

SHRUBS & VINES

Barberry, Creeping; Mahonia
Berberis repens
to 12", PO

Barberry, red, Algerita
Berberis haematocarpa
to 6', RS, MG

Blackberry, Himalaya
Rubus procerus, to 6',
naturalized in Oak Creek Canyon

Broom, desert
Baccharis sarothroides
to 10', RS

Buckthorn, California, Coffeeberry
Rhamnus californica
to 10', or more, PO, RP

Buckthorn, Hollyleaf; Coffeeberry
Rhamnus crocea
to 15', PO

Catclaw acacia
Acacia greggii
to 23', often smaller, MG, RS

Ceanothus, Desert
Ceanothus greggii
to 8', MG, PJ

Cliff-rose
Purshia mexicana
to 8', MG, PJ, RS

Creosote bush
Larrea tridentata
to 10', MG

Dalea, Feather
Dalea formosa
to 16", MG, RS

Ephedra, Longleaf; Desert jointleaf
Ephedra trifuca
to 4', MG

Fern, Bracken
Pteridium aquilinum
to 4', PO

Grape, Canyon
Vitis arizonica,
spreading vine, RP

Gray Thorn
Ziziphus obtusifolia
to 10', Rp

Ivy, Poison
Toxicodendron radicans; climbing
vine, variable leaf shapes, RP

Manzanita, Pointleaf
Arctostaphylos pungens
to 6', RS, PO

Oak, Scrub
Quercus turbinella
to 13', RS

Saltbush, Four-wing
Atriplex canescens
to 8', PJ, PO

Sugarbush, Sugar Sumac
Rhus ovata
to 15', RS

Wait-a-minute Bush
Mimosa biuncifera
to 8', MG, RS

When conditions are right, springtime brings white and pale lavender froths of Ceanothus blossoms along area trails. Then the air is as fragrant as a bridal bower.

MG = mesquite/grasslands **RP** = riparian (near water) **RS** = chaparral/rocky slopes **PJ** - pinyon/juniper **PO** - pine/oak **SF** spruce/fir

Alder, Arizona
Alnus oblongifolia
to 60', RP

Ash, Velvet
Fraxinus veluntina
to 30', RP

Boxelder
Acer negundo
to 50', RP

Cottonwood, Fremont
Populus fremontii
to 100', RP

Crucifixion Thorn
Canotia holacantha
to 12', MG, RS

Cypress, Arizona smooth-bark
Cupressus glabra
to 40', RS

Fir, Douglas
Pseudotsuga menziesii
100' or more, SF, PO

Hackberry, Netleaf
Celtis reticulata
to 30', RP, RS

Juniper, Alligator
Juniperus deppeana
20'-40', PJ, PO

Juniper, one-seed
Juniperus monosperma to 25′, multi-
trunked, low branches, PJ, MG

Juniper, Utah
Juniperus osteosperma
to 20′, bigger trunks, PJ, MG

Locust, New Mexico
Robinia neomexicana
to 25′, RP, PO

Maple, Bigtooth
Acer grandidentatum
to 35′, RP

Mesquite, Velvet
Prosopis velutina
to 30′, MG, RP

Oak, Arizona white
Quercus Arizonica
to 60′, PO

Oak, Emery
Quercus emoryi
to 50′, RP, RS

Oak, Gambel
Quercus gambelii
to 50′, PO

Pine, Pinyon
Pinus edulis
to 30′, PJ

MG = mesquite/grasslands **RP** = riparian (near water) **RS** = chaparral/rocky slopes **PJ** - pinyon/juniper **PO** - pine/oak **SF** spruce/fir

Pine, Ponderosa
Pinus ponderosa
to 125', PO

Sumac, Smooth
Rhus glabra
to 20', PO

Sycamore, Arizona
Planatus wrightii
to 80', RP

Walnut, Arizona black
Juglans major
to 45', RP

Willow, Desert
Chilopsis linearis
to 25', RP, MG

Willow, Goodding's
Salix gooddingii
to 45', RP

You are within five minutes from the forest in almost any part of Sedona.

CACTI & DESERT PLANTS

Beargrass
Nolina microcarpa
to 8', RS

Century Plant; Agave
Agave parryi
to 20', RS

Cactus, Claret cup Hedgehog
Echinocereus triglochidiatus
to 20", RS

Cactus, Prickly pear
Opuntia engelmannii
to 5', MG, PJ, RS

Cactus, Strawberry Hedgehog
Echinocereus engelmannii
to 16", RS

Cholla, Whipple
Cylindropuntia whipplei
to 3', MG

Yucca, Banana
Yucca baccata
to 5', MG, RS

Yucca, Soaptree
Yucca elata
to 30', MG

MG = mesquite/grasslands **RP** = riparian (near water) **RS** = chaparral/rocky slopes **PJ** - pinyon/juniper **PO** - pine/oak **SF** spruce/fir

Left: *Riparian areas like this scene along Oak Creek are crowded with water-thirsty plants---and rich autumn hues.*

Bottom: *Rocky slopes are alive with insects, reptiles, mammals and birds.*

AUTUMN

A few flirtatious cottonwood trees flaunt a golden leaf or two in late August, but I'm not fooled. The foliage really begins to change in upper Oak Creek Canyon in mid-September. The gold slips down Oak Creek, bestowing its Midas touch below Cathedral Rock in late October. Oak trees, Arizona sycamores, Smooth sumac, Fremont cottonwoods, Goodding willows and more stitch a rich patchwork of rust, red, and ochre hues. Conifers add green accents.

The cool micro-climate of West Fork blazes with red and coral Bigtooth maples by about mid-October. That's just in time to buy jugs of hand-pressed cider from Oak Creek Canyon orchards at the weekend roadside stand. I savor the feasts for both eyes and taste buds.

Opposite: *In summer Slide Rock is a swimmer's delight; the rest of the year it is simply a visual banquet.*

Below: *Cliffs just below Slide Rock are framed by multi-colored leaves of an Arizona sycamore.*

Oak Creek isn't the only Verde Valley waterway brightened with kaleidoscope colors during autumn. Sycamore Canyon, Wet Beaver Creek, Clear Creek, and the Verde River provide great hiking with photo ops at every bend. Or walk/bird the golden trails at Page Springs Fish Hatchery, and enjoy the wine-tasting rooms along the same lovely road.

Above: *Cathedral Rock's spires reflect in a tiny pool.*

Left: *Arizona sycamores have a mottled bark that turns apple green when wet.*

Right: *A Bigtooth maple lights up the stream through West Fork.*

Fall can be perfect time for hiking, as it is often mild enough to tackle unshaded or steep trails that are too hot for summer. Mud and ice are politely waiting for winter. Perfect as the trails can be, both visitors and residents often become local headlines. Extraction by our Ropes that Rescue crew, or by helicopter, can painful, expensive, and preventable.

Even a sprained ankle can incapacitate you. Tell someone your destination. Hike with a buddy. Stay on system trails. Carry water, energy bars, a cell phone, a flashlight for signaling, and warm clothing against surprisingly cold nights. Better to carry items you won't need than to travel light and become a statistic. If lost, stay put after dark. But if you're well--prepared, there's a wonderland of trails to explore. Bring a camera!

Pages 44 & 45: *Uptown Sedona sits between Wilson Mountain and a sea of fall color from this Hwy. 179 viewpoint.*

Left: *A biker enjoys the Bell Rock section of Red Rock Pathway, which encircles Sedona. Though shown here in summer, the pathway is popular year-round.*

Above: *A wall of Fay Canyon dwarfs the Golf Tees, which are examples of hoodoo formations.*

Left: *The Kisva Trail is one of five short, lovely trails in Red Rock State Park on Lower Red Rock Loop Road.*

As autumn slowly winds its way through Oak Creek Canyon, Sedona, Red Rock Crossing, and Red Rock State Park, traces of it linger into December. Then the shadows on the sandstone cliffs subtly become cooler, and the blue of the sky takes on a dancing, crystalline depth. The night sky, ever a thrill in Sedona's clear air, is radiant with starlight. Though I am sorry to see the last leaf fall, scores of birds are returning, and the delights of winter await.

Left: *In late October only fall color dips its toes into this Oak Creek swimming hole.*

Below: *West Fork's Bigtooth maples create a coral blizzard among the conifers.*
With B. Clemenz

Right: *Riparian trees along Oak Creek brighten this view east from the end of Uptown Sedona.*

Sedona has some wildlife species that are less commonly seen in other states and countries. Yes, we have rodents, rabbits, squirrels, raccoons, Mule deer, Black bears, and rarely, even mountain lions. This chapter features a few creatures associated with or unique to the southwest. Always give them enough distance so that they don't feel threatened.

Gray fox, up to 41" long
A canine, the Gray fox is a beautiful animal weighing from 7 to 14 pounds. Its thick fur is salt-and-pepper colored with rust and black accents. They are active by day and into night in mountains, forests, and broken terrain. Some have rabies.

Javelina (Collared peccary,) to 4' long
Like a flattened pig with wire-brush fur, javelinas (have-a-LEE-na) roam in groups, seeking cacti, succulents, bulbs, tubers, and dropped fruit or nuts. Plant these, and they will come! Not pigs, they belong to the peccary family of Central and South America. They have poor vision, stinky scent glands, straight, sharp tusks, and can be aggressive around food sources, including bird seed and pet food. They use drainages and dense brush as travel corridors. They are mostly, but not always, nocturnal.

Otter, up to 48" long *Settlers eradicated river otters in Arizona in the early 1900s. Twenty of them were reintroduced to the Verde River in 1981, and fortunately have flourished, spreading up Oak Creek and other area drainages. These playful creatures are mostly active at night. Their dens are in river banks, or under rocks and debris. Fortunately their diets include crawfish, an invasive, widespread species.*

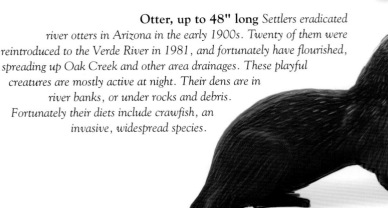

Above: *Sedona's cliffs, forests, grasslands, and riparian areas provide shelter, food and water for many creatures. Even Prickly Pear cactus pads are eaten by javelina. Their flowers provide nectar for insects and hummingbirds.*

Ringtail, about 30", including tail

Ringtails are the state mammal of Arizona. Cousins of the raccoon, ringtails differ in their small, slender bodies, short hair, huge eyes and ears, and a bushy black-and-white striped tail as long as their 17" bodies. Like raccoons, which also occur here, they are nocturnal. Ringtails prefer rocky terrain and often nest in trees.

Coyote, up to 49" long

This relative of the domesticated dog is often seen and heard. Unlike domestic dogs, it carries its bushy tail low. The night song of Arizona is the overlapping "yip-yip-yip" calls of a group of coyotes on the prowl. They can be seen day or night at any elevation and any habitat, including neighborhoods. Small domestic pets are definitely on their menu.

Bobcat, up to 33"

Related to the lynx, this spotted cat is most active dawn and dusk in all habitats, including neighborhoods. Its fur can have a yellowish or rusty hue with rusty spots. They are usually solitary.

Spotted skunk, up to 17" long

Striped skunks, with their nose-to-tail white stripe are common in other states, but the Spotted skunk prevails in Arizona and Sedona. It has various white stripes on its body and tail. Spotted skunks are often near water sources. They are nocturnal omnivores that can emit an awful odor, and are prone to rabies. Cute though they are, give them their distance!

Painted Lady

Two-tailed Swallowtail

Monarch

Of the 330 species of butterflies in Arizona, Sedona has a generous share. Three of the most common are illustrated.

Butterflies of Arizona by Stewart, Brodkin and Brodkin is an essential field guide.

A. B. C. D. E.

Arthropods have external skeletons and no central vertebra. Worms, insects, and butterflies are among numerous Arthropods. Watch out for the more dangerous ones described here. Many are seldom seen, but knowledge prepares you if you do meet up. Keep the booklet *Poisonous Dwellers of the Desert*[1] in your backpack. Carry a small flashlight. Don't ever put fingers, feet, or other body parts in places too dark, too high, or too low to see clearly!

A. Black Widow spider *Wood piles, rock cracks, old rodent holes, and under debris, rocks and logs are hiding places, as are garages, barns, and attics. Don't reach into dark places! If bitten, pain and symptoms are intense. Stop what you're doing and get medical help without delay.*

B. Centipedes *The fast-moving Giant centipede can be 6 to 8" long. They are mostly nocturnal, and prefer leaf litter, crevices, rocks, and wood. They have two pincers plus sharp leg claws that can pierce skin and soft leather. People allergic to bee stings need medical attention. Most people just experience pain.*

C. Kissing bug (Cone-nose bug) *Blood-sucking Kissing bugs are an inch long or less. They are parasitic to wood rats and voles. Rodent dens, bright night lighting, and house openings are invitations to Kissing bugs. At worst, they can cause anaphylactic shock requiring medical attention. Severe itching, including palms, soles of feet, and the groin often occur, as well as a large, hard, red welt and possible additional symptoms. Antibiotics may be needed. Reaction to bites can require medical care.*

D. Tarantula *Although most insects make me shudder, I think of these large, slow-moving spiders as small animals who can't quite coordinate their legs. They seldom bite unless really provoked. I once saw one walk hand-to-hand across the palms of squealing, delighted children at a nature talk. Consensus? "It tickles!" If tarantulas are provoked into biting, infection is possible and an antibiotic may be needed. Just leave them alone!*

E. Scorpions *The small, slender Bark scorpion is the most dangerous of Arizona scorpion species. Its body is slender (straight) rather than rounded, and it is about 2" long. Scorpions can climb rocks and walls. In dwellings it prefers sinks, tubs, bedding, and storage areas. If stung, babies, children under age four, and the elderly should seek immediate medical care. While the dangerous Bark scorpion lives primarily in southern Arizona and the Colorado River, stings from any scorpion are very painful and merit a call to a doctor or the Arizona Poison & Drug Information Center: 1-800-222-1222.*

1 By Natt Dodge

Mexican
Spadefoot Toad

Arizona's great variations in elevation and biological zones provide ideal habitats for many reptiles and some amphibians. The Sedona area has its fair share.

Snakes intrigue many visitors, either from fear or curiosity. Most snakes are harmless and not aggressive. The majority of snake bites in Arizona occur when people corner or try to drive off snakes. Reaching into debris, under rocks, ledges, and wood are other leading causes. Usually backing off, staying calm, and letting a snake get away is the safest option. Wearing shoes rather than sandals can protect vulnerable feet.

Not all diamond-patterned snakes are rattlers. My semi--rural Sedona street had a Gopher snake for years. Once it chased a mouse from bush to bush as I was sipping wine on my patio at dusk. Another time it bulged motionless on the ground from having just ingested a gopher. It was a soft butter yellow with diamond-shaped blotches, and was appreciated for gopher control. Area snakes hibernate during colder months

Sedona lizards range from slim and small to longer, huskier Collared lizards, but none are aggressive. You'll see the occasional frog, especially at marshy and stream banks.

Great Basin Collared Lizard

Desert Grassland Whiptail Lizard

A few species you might see without trying include:

Snakes *About half of Arizona's 13 rattlesnake species occur in the greater Sedona area. All have a broad, heart-shaped head, and usually shake their rattles if alarmed. If bitten, tourniquets or suction are no longer advised. Immobilize the limb, elevate it above heart level, go to a hospital or call 911. Do not delay! If possible, take a photo of the snake to optimize the anti-venom choice. Minimize risk outdoors by not reaching where you can't see. Because prey such as mice seek water sources, snakes sometimes frequent waterways to hunt for food. Always use a flashlight at night during warmer months.*

Lizards *Of the 49 Arizona lizard species, 18 are found in the area. Desert Grassland whiptails and Plateau Fence lizards are commonly seen in nature and around buildings. The Eastern collared lizard is bigger, colorful critter. If you hear the shaking of dry leaves on the forest floor, it is often lizards rummaging for food. Lizards and toads can be toxic to dogs – so keep your pet within sight and check it frequently.*

Toads and frogs *The area hosts 5 toad species (bumpy, drier skin, mostly terrestrial), and 7 frog species (moister, smooth skin, mostly aquatic.)*

Regal Horned Lizard

Above: *Reptiles often bask on the sandstone to raise their body temperatures. They can scoot to the shade of rocks or forests for protection or cooling.*

Western Dimondback Rattlesnake

The American culture prevalent in Sedona and Verde Valley today is only the most recent to call this area home. Carbon dating of pictographs at Palatki Ruins, and artifacts found in Sycamore Canyon suggest that humans were here 5,000 years ago.

The Hohokams, 600 - 1000 A.D., built irrigation ditches for their fields from the outflow of Montezuma Well. The ditches are still in use. The Sinagua, 1100 - 1400 A.D., were also farmers. Their pit house homes evolved to complex masonry villages like those at Montezuma Castle and Tuzigoot National Monuments. These were abandoned about 1400. Many ruins and artifacts remain.

Spanish explorer Antonio de Espejo visited the Verde Valley in 1583 and found the masonry villages unoccupied and crumbling. Instead, the Yavapai, of Yuman language culture, and the Tonto Apaches, of the Athabascan language group, were peacefully co-existing. They hunted, gathered, farmed, and lived in temporary thatched dwellings. They mined rocks for tools, arrows, paint and jewelry, and traded with very distant cultures. Their descendents live just north of Camp Verde and in a small area in Clarkdale. The Anglo-American newcomers established Fort Lincoln, now Camp Verde, in 1871, decimating the native culture in many ways. The worst atrocity was the rounding up of 1500 Yavapais and Apaches and marching them 100 miles east to the San Carlos Reservation in the dead of winter. Those who didn't freeze or starve to death returned after 20 years and carved their own destiny. Today they operate a casino and other businesses in the area, and are good neighbors whose culture has earned admiration and respect.

Right: *The trail outside the well leads to an ancient irrigation canal dug centuries ago.*

Montezuma Well National Monument
Take I-17 exit 293 east, and follow signs. About 4 miles

It's a hot climb in summer to the rim of this 368' wide collapsed limestone cavern, which is 55' deep. There are Sinagua ruins dating from about 1150 A.D. under the rim and at the bottom of the trail to water level. The irrigation canal at the outside base of the Well dates to the earlier Hohokam culture.

There are Hohokam pit house ruins at a roadside marker driving in. Enjoy shaded picnics, birding, and rest rooms at right, driving in. No visitor center. Fee or parks pass.

Tuzigoot National Monument
Turnoff is on 89A between Old Town Cottonwood and Clarkdale.

Enjoy the great exhibits in the pueblo-style visitor center, then climb the slope to these 800 year old pueblo ruins. Read the signs by the ruins path explaining how native peoples used plants for food medicine, clothing and tools, Go inside the ruins and up top, as Sinagua sentries once did. This ridge-top village was entirely hidden by earth and plants before excavation in the 1930s. Pass or fee.

Montezuma Castle National Monument
Exit I-17 289 east 1/2 mile, then left at sign. Camp Verde

A short, paved walk along Wet Beaver Creek reveals a dramatic 20-room Sinagua dwelling 100' high in a white lime-stone cliff, and the ruins of a 45-room dwelling. Ruins are 12th and 13th century, and were misnamed by early discoverers. Don't miss the little diorama on the lower walk, and allow time to enjoy the visitor center displays and book store. Picnic tables, flush toilets, good RV access. Pass or fee.

Honanki Heritage Site (U.S. Forest Service)
From West Sedona, take Hwy. 89A southwest to F.R. 525. Turn north for 9.5 miles, bearing left after FR 795.
GPS: N34° 56' 19.032", W-111° 55' 59.9874"

From 1100 to 1300 the Sinagua people hunted, farmed, gleaned native plants for food and fibers, and created rock art here. They built dwellings in a place where we might quickly starve. Site stewards bring to life the history of these people from 9:00 a.m. to 4 p.m. daily except Thanksgiving and Christmas. Road can be very rough, rutted and rocky. Vault toilets. No water. Tour reservation and Red Rock Pass required.

Crescent Moon Ranch Day Use Area (Red Rock Crossing)

U.S. Forest Service *From W. Sedona, take 89A to Upper Red Rock Loop Rd. Turn left, then left again onto Chavez Ranch Rd. & follow signs.*

This park is included here because of its iconic view of Cathedral Rock reflected in Oak Creek. Enjoy hiking, swimming, picnicking, year-round photography and birding under tall sycamores and cottonwoods. Historic water wheel was part of pioneer ranching days. Reserve group ramada. Toilets, water. Fee.

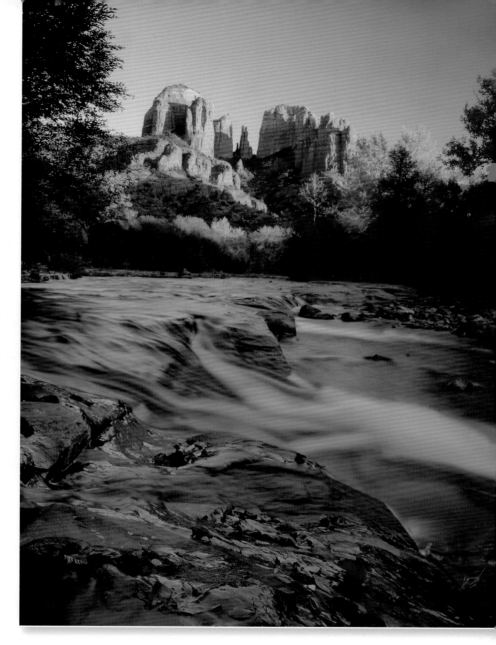

V Bar V Heritage Site

(U.S. Forest Service) *From I-17 take exit 298 east onto F.R. 618. At 2 miles the road bears right. Site is immediately at right.*

An astonishing sandstone wall crowded with petroglyphs awaits you after a 1/3 mile flat woodsy trail along Wet Beaver Creek. Docents explain 700 to 900 year old rock art. The only ruins is the original ranch house chimney. Visitor center, bookstore, toilets. Good birding. Open Thursday - Monday. 9:30 a.m. - 3 p.m. Red Rock Pass available here.

Palatki Heritage Site (U.S. Forest Service)

From West Sedona, take Hwy. 89A to F.R. 525. Turn north for 5 miles, then 2 mi. north on F.R. 795. GPS: N34° 54' 58.2474", W-111° 54' 6.228"

Magnificent Red Canyon preserves small ruins dating from 1100 - 1300. A rock cove on a trail west of the ruins contains rock art from all known ancient cultures. Resident site stewards lead tours every 20 minutes, 9:40 a.m. to 3 p.m. This is a memorable archeological site and setting.

Reservations required. Visitor center, toilets, water. Red Rock Pass required (sold here.)

Jerome State Historic Park (Douglas Mining Museum)

From Cottonwood take 89A toward Jerome. Turnoff is at milepost 345.

This beautiful home and museum depicts the copper mining boom town that was Jerome from the 1880s to the mid 1950s. The building was home to mining magnate James S. Douglas. Some rooms have period furnishings, others have fascinating displays, mine artifacts, mineral specimens, and a great movie of Jerome's boom-time history. Toilets, water, visitor center. Fee or State Parks pass.

Fort Verde State Historic Park

Take I-17 exit 287 southeast to Finnie Flats Rd. Turn left and follow into town. Park is on left.

This park is the best-preserved post-Civil War park in Arizona. It is a treasury of late 1800's cavalry life with authentic furnishings, artifacts, and military history. Tour the museum in the Headquarters Building and the fully furnished officer's and doctor's homes. Many events through the year. Closed Tuesdays & Wednesdays. Toilets, picnic area. Fee or State Parks pass.

Dead Horse Ranch State Park

From Cottonwood's Hwy. 260 & Hwy 89A junction, go north on 89A about 2 miles. Turn right on 10th St.

Bring your kids, your horses, your kayak, and your tent or RV to this large park on the Verde River. Activities includes hiking, fishing, birding and picnics (including group ramada.) Rent a heated, cooled sleep cabin. Attend the annual birding festival (end of April) or Verde River Day (late September.) Toilets, showers, hookups, horse corral, dump station, visitor center. Reserve facilities. State Parks pass or fees.

Red Rock State Park
Take 89A from West Sedona to Lower Red Rock Loop Rd.
Turn left and drive about 2 miles.

This 286 acre park straddles Oak Creek. Environmental education is the park's purpose. Enjoy 5 miles of hiking trails, group and individual picnic areas, a visitor center with natural and cultural history, a movie theater, frequent birding and nature walks, bird feeders, and a nest site for the Common Black Hawk. Water, toilets, a book/gift shop, and green architecture. Fee or State Parks Pass.

Slide Rock State Park
From uptown Sedona, go north 8 miles on
Hwy. 89A to park entrance on left.

There's still a working orchard at this former Pendley family farm. The home, apple packing barn, and farm equipment remain. The big attraction, though, is slippery, submerged sandstone ledges that channel Oak Creek's water, zipping swimmers down a series of drops. Wear cut-off jeans over your swim suit to prevent skin abrasions and exposed fannies. No pets in car or swim area. Bring a picnic but no glass. No soiled diapers in creek. Toilets, water, small seasonal store for snacks, sunscreen, etc. Arrive early to avoid entrance delays. State Parks pass or fee.

Clemenceau Heritage Museum, Cottonwood
Corner of N. Willard & E. Mingus

This old school building houses exhibits of an historic classroom, home interiors from the early 20th century, and actual items and photographs of the Verde Valley's 19th century mining, ranching and farming days. The museum's model train room has fascinating, detailed dioramas of Verde Valley historic scenes with model trains running through them. Volunteers open the museum Wednesdays through Sundays. Check **clemenceaumuseum.com** for hours.

Sedona Historical Museum
North end of Jordan Rd. in uptown Sedona

The Sedona Heritage Museum is an authentic little gem that is housed in the original sandstone home of Walter and Ruth Jordan, Sedona pioneers and orchardists. Their barn and its equipment is also preserved, as is the movie set Telegraph Office from Sedona's Western film-making heydays. Some exhibits are permanent, some change, and there are events at least three times monthly. Check out **sedonamuseum.org**. Children under 13 admitted free.

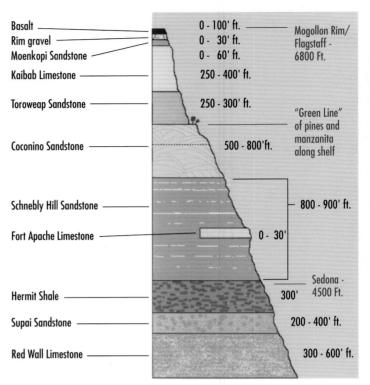

Layer	Thickness	Notes
Basalt	0 - 100' ft.	Mogollon Rim/ Flagstaff - 6800 Ft.
Rim gravel	0 - 30' ft.	
Moenkopi Sandstone	0 - 60' ft.	
Kaibab Limestone	250 - 400' ft.	
Toroweap Sandstone	250 - 300' ft.	"Green Line" of pines and manzanita along shelf
Coconino Sandstone	500 - 800' ft.	
Schnebly Hill Sandstone	800 - 900' ft.	
Fort Apache Limestone	0 - 30'	Sedona - 4500 Ft.
Hermit Shale	300'	
Supai Sandstone	200 - 400' ft.	
Red Wall Limestone	300 - 600' ft.	

Graph courtesy of arizonaruins.com/sedona

Sedona's rock layers and eroded shapes are more complex than their coloration is. Sedona geologist Paul Lindberg has provided this summary of how Sedona got from there to here. Other resources are listed on page 2. The graph above of Sedona's rock strata provides names for geologic deposits. For simplification, the acronym "MYA," meaning "million years ago, is used here rather than geologic era names.

1,800 to 1,600 MYA

During the late Precambrian Era volcanic islands and sedimentary basins existed off the coast of ancestral North America. By 1,700 MYA tectonic forces had compressed, folded and added those rocks to form Arizona's oldest landmass. Deeply eroded former mountain ranges ("basement rocks") extend under most of North America. They are exposed in Arizona beneath younger cover rocks in the bottom of the Grand Canyon, and in the Prescott and Jerome areas.

1,200 to 550 MYA

Following a long period of erosion the land began to subside, and deposition of new river-borne sediments covered the older basement rocks. Renewed tectonic forces generated fault-bounded and tilted mountain ranges, but by 550 MYA those former mountains were again reduced by erosion to a nearly flat plane. The roots of those late Precambrian highlands are exposed in the bottom of the eastern Grand Canyon and north of Chino Valley near Prescott.

The allure of Sedona's beauty lies in its geology, or, more specifically, from trace amounts of rust! Yes, iron oxide pigmentation gives some of the sedimentary layers in the cliffs above town the spectacular red-orange color we commonly called "red rocks."

Above: Supai Sandstone from the late Paleozoic period is visible south of Midgely Bridge. *Far left:* A Fay Canyon crevice is eroding away, collecting enough soil, water and nutrients to support a pinyon tree. *Left:* Sandstone disks 7' across have tumbled from Red Canyon's wall and will weather away to sand.

550 to 250 MYA

Between 550 and 250 MYA the land continued to subside as sediments were deposited onto the continental margin, just below or just above sea level. That succession of Paleozoic Era sedimentary rocks forms the flat-lying beds exposed in the upper two-thirds of the Grand Canyon. Within that thick pile of sedimentary rocks is Redwall Limestone, composed of the skeletal remains of marine shells. These were deposited when Arizona's land mass was near the Equator. At that time North America was drifting northward at roughly the same rate that our fingernails grow. Wind-blown quartz sand dunes then capped the limestone beds to form the buff-colored Coconino Sandstone layer that lies above Sedona's red rocks. Those strata are in turn capped by the Kaibab Limestone that forms both rims of the Grand Canyon and the apex of Wilson Mountain north of Sedona. The upper third of this Paleozoic sedimentary succession can be seen in the Mogollon Rim cliffs above Sedona.

In 1869, Grand Canyon explorer John Wesley Powell noticed a gap in the geologic record. Cambrian Period Tapeats Sandstone from 550 MYA was laid down right on top of ancient eroded Precambrian basement rocks from 1,700 to 1,800 MYA, but deposits from the intervening eras are missing throughout Northern Arizona. Powell named this "the Great Unconformity." It is visible above the United Verde open pit mine in Jerome.

By 250 MYA most of the world's continental plates had been fused together to form the supercontinent called Pangea. The Mesozoic Era that followed has been called the Age of Reptiles. Within the next 50 MYA the more familiar continental outlines began to take shape as the supercontinent began breaking apart. During the warm, ice-free Cretaceous Period 100 MYA, ocean level was at an all-time high. A seaway extended unbroken from the Gulf of Mexico to the Arctic Ocean. It passed through northeastern Arizona, separating North America into two landmasses. By about 70 MYA the sea had retreated from the region for the last geologically recorded time.

70 to 15 MYA

By roughly 70 MYA the west-moving North American continental plate began to collide with the east-moving Farallon oceanic plate. Denser oceanic rocks began to plunge beneath the thicker and lighter continental rocks, raising the landmass in the process. Over millions of years the rock strata of the Southwestern U.S. was slowly raised to create the Colorado Plateau. Faulting allowed for some continental blocks to be raised higher than their neighbors. The highest terrain created by the Laramide mountain building event lay in Arizona's Central Highlands, well outboard of today's eroded edge of the Colorado Plateau. Northeastward-directed stream flow eroded younger sedimentary rocks from the Prescott region and exposed ancient Precambrian bedrock in that area.

Exotic gravels bearing Precambrian rock clasts, called Rim Gravels, were carried onto the surface of the plateau over a wide area. This is because the uplifted terrain had been reduced to a shallow-dipping erosional surface. That surface drained from the Central Highlands toward the northeast, onto what we today call the Colorado Plateau. Near the end of this time period volcanic eruptions deposited lavas on top of the gravel beds and truncated the Paleozoic rock surface. Mingus Mountain near Jerome, House Mountain near Sedona, and the Colorado Plateau basalt lava flows contain caprocks composed of young lava flows.

*Devil's Bridge (**top left**) and Vultee Arch (**bottom**) off Dry Creek Road's dirt section are obvious arches. Nearby Fay Canyon Arch (**top right**) has separated from the canyon wall only by 12 feet, and is hard to spot.*

15 MYA to present day

By 15 MYA the Earth's crustal rocks across much of the western United States were being pulled apart and thinned. The downward pull of the deeply-buried Farallon oceanic plate helped create the basin and range physiographic province. By 8 to 10 MYA ago crustal extension had progressed into the Verde valley region, creating the Chino and Verde grabens (rift valleys.) Core rocks of the Verde graben, lying between Sedona and Jerome and verified by deep drill holes, were dropped in excess of 6100 feet. Remnants of the former plateau surface remain as high-standing horsts, such as Mingus Mountain near Jerome and Wilson Mountain above Sedona. Dramatic regional drainage reversals began to erode the margins of the Verde and other nearby depressions. These eventually filled the closed basins with gravel and brackish water limestone beds. The Mogollon Rim erosional escarpment was then formed along the northeastern side of the structural basins.

Sedona's beautifully sculpted cliffs morphed into their present form only in the last 8 million years. Their presence here is a gift as inspiring and fleeting as a rainbow after a summer monsoon storm.

Top: *Merry-Go-Round Rock on Schnebly Hill gives a close-up view of the very visible 10' thick gray Fort Apache Limestone band on cliffs around Sedona.*

Right: *Sinkholes such as Devil's Kitchen are created when underlying limestone dissolves.*

Bottom: *Coconino Sandstone's light tan colors top Fin Rock (shown,) and West Sedona's Capitol Butte, and are also visible high in Oak Creek Canyon and Schnebly Hill.*

WINTER

Winter is mild in Sedona. The average annual snowfall is a mere 8 inches. Keep your hiking boots and birding binoculars ready, as you can use them more days than not. In fact, scores of northern bird species bypass the frigid Colorado Plateau and happily winter here. Hikers head for the sunny trails that can be a titch hot in the summer: Long Canyon, Courthouse Loop, the system around Cathedral Rock, nearby Bell Trail by Wet Beaver Creek, trails in Cottonwood's Dead Horse Ranch State Park – there are too many to name. Reptiles hibernate from about November through March, another plus.

In winter Sedona is alive with an international-caliber chamber music series, a major film festival, a marathon, a Saint Patrick's Day parade, and other entertainments. Ask to tag along with the archeology club, with Northern Arizona Audubon birding club, or with the Sedona Westerners hiking club. Bundle up on clear nights for views of the universe with area astronomy clubs. You'll find that locals tend to be friendly and welcoming.

Right: Catching Cathedral Rock with sunlit snow down to creek level is a rare treat.
Below: Page Springs Fish Hatchery (shown) and the Sedona Wetlands Preserve offer great winter birding.
Next page: The Pallisades look majestic with a quick-melting mantle of snow.

Now and then Jack Frost waves his magic wand and Sedonans awaken to a baby blanket of snow. It usually disappears by mid-morning and thoughtfully doesn't even stick to the streets. More rarely, snow falls on two or three consecutive days. Then, as the clouds lift, the sunlight turns them to a radiant silver, and euphoric people step outside and dance! The other-world majesty of the snow-etched red cliffs confirms what Sedonans often suspect: This, indeed, is Camelot.

Above: *Clearing snow clouds surround Courthouse Rock "for one brief, shining moment."*

Of course winter has its moments. Heavy rainfall above the Rim can melt the Plateau's occasionally deep snow pack, and torrents of snarling red water careen down Oak Creek. Even normally dry arroyos can dislodge cars, mobile homes, heavy debris and large trees.. Many a big SUV or 4WD pickup truck has ended up totaled from a driver's over-confidence. If you ignore flood barricades or signs, Arizona's "Stupid Motorist Law" can kick in with fines to cover your rescue costs. Risky, embarrassing, life-threatening! Turn around or wait out the flood. Summer monsoons can have the same consequences.

Above: *Snowmelt thunders through the normally quiet waters of Oak Creek at Slide Rock State Park.*

Top: *Pumphouse Wash below Oak Creek Canyon's switchbacks sparkles with snow.*

Middle: *Trails in the Coffee Pot Rock and Soldier Pass areas can be great to hike in winter.*

Right: *This snowy scene of the Red Rock - Secret Mountain area had only traces of snow two days later.*

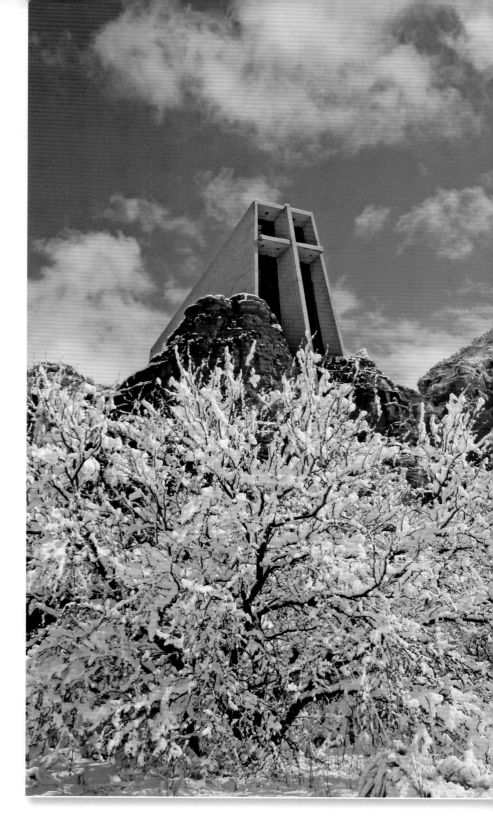

So what to do on inclement days? The art galleries, shops and restaurants in Uptown Sedona, Tlaquepaque, and the Gallery District offer lots of diversions. Check newspaper entertainment guides for movies, plays, and other performances. Enjoy the displays and movies and chat with docents or rangers at visitor centers operated by the U.S. Forest Service, the state parks, national monuments, and Sedona Heritage Museum. Spend a few hours on the sofas by the fireplace and tall windows at the magnificent Sedona Public Library just off Dry Creek Road. The architecture alone merits a visit.

Head to Cottonwood's Old Town and stroll under authentic Old West covered walkways, visiting wine-tasting rooms, shops, and great restaurants. Do the same up the hill in Jerome. Ride on Clarkdale's excursion train through the red sandstone Verde River Canyon and watch the eagles soar and the javelinas high-tail it.

The bonus for winter visitors? You'll avoid the much busier April through December seasons. Do remember that this chapter shows the rare, beautiful snowy days that most visitors don't happen to see. Most days sparkle.

Right: *The dramatic Chapel of the Holy Cross faces south to views of Courthouse and Bell Rocks.*

Sedona residents often consider it a gift to live in a place that perhaps should have become a national park. It's a daily joy to live with the wonders, big and small, of the seasons: the ever-changing light on the red rocks, the richness of the plant and animal life, the appreciation of the cultures who lived here before us, and the vibrance of Sedona's community life. Seeing the smiles of discovery on the faces of visitors reminds Sedonans that it wasn't too long ago that we stood in your shoes.

Right: Capitol Butte in West Sedona glows in the last light of a winter day.

Below: The snow hardly settled on this cottonwood's branches before the morning sun began to nudge it off.

VERDE VALLEY VISTAS

There are other roadless red rock canyons in the Verde Valley. Verde River, Wet Beaver Creek, and Clear Creek canyons have perennial streams; Sycamore Canyon's creek runs only in the winter. The Verde Valley has parks, campgrounds, and major archeological sites. Camp Verde dates from cavalry days. Jerome, formerly a copper mining boom town, now mixes history with charming shops and cafes. Cottonwood's Old Town is alive with antique stores, unique restaurants, shops, wine-tasting, and historic covered sidewalks. Hike, bird, or ride horses on 100 miles of Valley trails, or ride the rails through beautiful Verde River Canyon.

The Sedona - Verde Valley area is rich in natural, cultural, and recreational wonders. Even a lifetime is hardly enough time to discover them all. Give it a try. Beware: visitors often catch "red rock fever." The cure is foolproof: frequent return visits to this beautiful, bountiful area.

Below: *It's lovely to kayak the Verde River from Camp Verde south to Beasely Flat. Birders and picnickers can enjoy the same route by land, taking Salt Mine Road south to Beasely Flat.*

Above: *North of Clarkdale the Verde River winds through a basalt gorge below blossoming ocotillo. Bald and Golden eagles often fly through this gorge or perch in the Fremont cottonwoods. The rocks change to red sandstone a few miles north at the confluence of Sycamore Canyon and Verde River Canyon.*

Clockwise from left: Douglas Mansion at Jerome State Historic Park with Mogollon Rim on horizon. Jerome viewed through mine cars at Douglas Mansion. Black Hills beyond lagoon at Dead Horse Ranch State Park. Fall color on the Verde River near Clarkdale.

Above: The swimming hole by Beaver Creek campground reflects the rusts and golds of Arizona sycamores.

Right: The excursion train from Clarkdale winds through the red sandstone cliffs of Verde River Canyon.

Pages 80 - 81: Sunset over Courthouse and Bell Rocks. With Bob C.

Back cover: Soaptree yucca blossoms frame Courthouse Rock.